THE
NEXT WORLD

THE
NEXT WORLD

CHRISTIEN
GHOLSON

SHANTI ARTS PUBLISHING

BRUNSWICK, MAINE

THE NEXT WORLD

Published by Shanti Arts Publishing

Designed by Shanti Arts Designs

Cover image: Clark Walding, *Distant View*, 1992.
Oil and wax over color montype. 44 x 44 inches
(111.7 x 111.7 cm). Used with permission of the artist.
www.clarkwalding.com / www.charlottejackson.com

Shanti Arts LLC
193 Hillside Road
Brunswick, Maine 04011
shantiarts.com

Printed in the United States of America

ISBN: 978-1-962082-43-3 (softcover)

Library of Congress Control Number: 2024951871

For Michaela

. . . I keep looking for

that snow, that space between flakes, that thought-
dissolving silence—under rocks, between furrows of

bark, in mist, tufts of dry grass, in the mirror. You keep
looking for it, too. We look for it together in our own

way, grey-eyed children of snow, of the ghosts of snow,
slowly becoming snow-ghosts ourselves, shadows that

appear at the corner of the eye . . .

Contents

Acknowledgments 9

Tarantula Migration on Highway 140,
  Near the Oregon-Nevada Line 11
Resurrection Ferns: Spells 12
I Open the Small Charred 13
Lit Blue 15
What Holds Everything Together 18
Protozoa, A Cave Painter, A Moth's Tongue:
  How the World Was Made 19
Ancestors, Early Winter Night 20
Starry Night over the Rhone (Vincent van Gogh) 21
Where Do the Bees Go? 22
The Hand inside the Pumpkin 23
A Snake, A Root, A Shoelace:
  How the World Was Made 24
Ancestor, At the Edge of Sleep 25
Crossing Western Wyoming Smothered
  in Forest Fire Smoke 27
Self-Portrait (Rembrandt) 28
Stilling: Red-Tailed Hawk 30
Our Mother's Body 32
The Rest of the Body 35
Refugee 36
Glaze Event: How the World Was Made 37
Ancestors, Out There 38
Nacer de Nuevo/Rebirth (Remedios Varo) 40
Low 41
Car Batteries, Falling Snow, Snakestones 42
Something Inside (Dreadful Euphoria) 43

Inside Leonora Carrington's Painting *The Giantess*
While Standing at the Edge of a Pond 44

What's Not There Calls to Me 46

Snow Clouds, Space, and Snow-Ghosts:
How the World Was Made 47

Ancestors, Day of the Dead 49

Sounding: How the World Was Made 51

Two Turkey Vultures: Early Spring 52

Bees, Faeries, Souls of the Dead, Maitake Mushrooms:
How the World Was Made 54

Watching Apricot Blossoms Fly during a Time of Plague 55

Dragonfly in the Palm 57

Blue Pool at Tamolitch Falls 60

The Autumn People 61

Moth Hovering between Two Incense Cedars 63

Jésus-Christ Nous Offrant Son Sang
(Gustave van de Woestyne) 64

Stone Shrieks, Birthday Balloons, Wind Sickness:
How the World Was Made 66

The Disappeared 67

Reprieve 69

Mourning 70

Oracular Melodies 71

Ancestor, Bringing the World Continually into Being 72

Rain, The Ceaseless Sea, The Water Works Drowned,
and Prophesy: How the World Was Made 73

What Is Crow (Polyphony) 75

Cairn: Earth and Mother 76

Ancestors 86

Notes 89

About the Author 93

Acknowledgments

Banyan Review: "Car Batteries, Falling Snow, Snakestones"; "I Open the Small Charred"; "Protozoa, a Cave Painter, a Moth's Tongue: How the World Was Made"; "Refugee"

The Bear Review: "Ancestor, Bringing the World into Being"

Cholla Needles: "Ancestors"; "Ancestors, Early Winter Night"; "Ancestors, Out There"; "The Autumn People"; "Blue Pool at Tamolitch Falls"; "The Disappeared"; "Lit Blue"; "Something Inside (Dreadful Euphoria)"; "Stilling: Red-Tailed Hawk"

Cirque: "Bees, Faeries, Souls of the Dead, Maitake Mushrooms: How the World Was Made"

Ekphrastic Review: "Inside Leonora Carrington's Painting *The Giantess* While Standing at the Edge of a Pond"; "Jésus-Christ Nous Offrant Son Sang (Gustave van de Woestyne)"; "Nacer de Nuevo/Rebirth (Remedios Varo)"

Fireweed: "Low"; "Tarantula Migration on Highway 140, Near the Oregon-Nevada Line"

Flyway: Writing & Environment: "Rain, The Ceaseless Sea, The Water Works Drowned, and Prophesy: How the World Was Made"; "What is Crow (Polyphony)"

Mudlark: "Dragonfly in the Palm"; "The Rest of the Body"; "Two Turkey Vultures: Early Spring"

Sheila-na-gig: "A Snake, A Root, A Shoelace: How the World Was Made"

The Shore: "What Holds Everything Together"

Tiger Moth Review: "Resurrection Ferns: Spells"; "What's Not There Calls to Me"

Wilderness House Review: "Where Do the Bees Go"; "Starry Night over the Rhone (Vincent van Gogh)"; "Self-Portrait (Rembrandt)"

Tarantula Migration on Highway 140, Near the Oregon-Nevada Line

1

The way ahead was thick with black crawling spider-bodies
the size of mice. And long black slicks where other cars had

spread them across the macadam. A shiver ran through me,
an electric cascade responding to the horror and thrill of seeing

so many males tracking pheromones, destined to mate and
sometimes be eaten. I laughed, thinking how the words "sacrifice"

and "fate"—such monstrously huge words to me—float so small
and inconsequential inside those bodies, where kernels of hydro-

gen and helium dust search across vast spaces for other kernels of
hydrogen and helium dust.

2

To the southwest, I thought I saw the ruin of some old ranch or
house. A crumbling wood monument I imagined built by some

American robber baron, still lurking inside, skeletal, muscles
able to cling to brittle bone because of the strength of his hubris,

believing he has the power to beckon the spiders towards him,
the way he used to have the power to alter lives and economies.

I see him watching as the spiders march past the ruins, following
their million-year-old path over the earth's rough skin, sending a

soft shiver of electricity into stone, sand—the euphoric sensation
of the earth recognizing itself.

Resurrection Ferns: Spells

They grow from moss on the oak's bark, dangle
twenty feet above the earth. Fronds like seawrack;
like sea-spells, drawing a ghost-ocean closer, closer,
for 70 million years, beneath this highway bridge.

I was a drop of rain, once; slipped down the length
of this oak's trunk for sixty years; years pilgrimed
inside phosphorescent labyrinths of moss, drawn up
steep xylem trails, tranced inside a sporangia patch.

I was part of this sea-spell, a drop; part of this sea-snake
spell, a spore; part of this sea-spell, a frond's memory
of a previous life as rain, a drop, that contained a sea
turtle turning around the oak's crown.

What is born again? I press my forehead against bark
and exhale. Transpiration draws salt water up through
the vascular trails of my body, from an ancient ocean,
a future ocean . . .

I Open the Small Charred

1

Rain all night. Mist dissolves the mountains.
I open the small, charred metal box you sent,

burnt 40 years ago in the house fire, and smell
that smell, so familiar, one that's always with me,

the smell of all-things-burning-at-once, mix of
meat executed at the stake and toxic paint-shrieks

in a vat of melted plastic, that still clings to things
inside the box—pieces of a lost life, one I tried to

erase from memory, because I could not contain
the loneliness we all shared inside that house.

2

The mountains emerge from nothing, as if they
were never gone. We never did recover from that

fire, did we? No one ever said it was something
we needed to recover from. *It happens all the time.*

Move on. Your life is ahead of you. What does
recover even mean? A return to a previous state.

I never wanted to make that return. The smell
clings to an old cartoon a child made to make

someone laugh. Anyone. Smoke-residue was
on that child's fingers long before the fire . . .

3

Outside, the oak is fire; amber, brick and blood
red. The brown along each leaf-edge is a glorious

life-shout inside a masque for death, while the
world all around this town will not recover from

last year's fires, or next year's fires (slowly
closing in). I take in a deep breath of that distant

burning, close the lid, knowing where I can find
it anytime, inside this small, charred box, that I've

given the impossible task of holding everything
that cannot be contained.

Lit Blue

1

The sun's red, sore, soaked in forest ash. Ash words,
blood particulates. The terrible sky is now routine, so

I sleep all day, scour recycling bins at night. There are
atrocities down here at ground-level: bodies everywhere.

I see them: a hand dangling outside a rain-soaked blanket
by the river, a face hidden in a sea of bulging plastic bags.

They appear and disappear according to the angle of light.
I rattle. I am the rain. There's the comforting smell of worms

from the grime in my fingernails. I am soil. I am the earth.
Why will no one look at me, say thank you? I am the sound

of bike tires while the city weaves its own shroud, all windows
lit blue from computer screen light. Ambulances pass silently,

hunting for bodies. Police cars pass, hunting for bodies.

2

Who will know when I die, who will whisper that fact to
someone else? I remember there was a hurricane when my

father died. All electricity gone, so we put bags of frozen
vegetables around the body until the funeral home could show.

When they finally arrived two days later—a father and son—
I told them there were bags of frozen vegetables beneath

the body. The father looked at me, confused, said: "Do you
want them back?" "No, no, I'm just telling you what's

underneath him, in case that matters for cremation." It didn't.
I tell the story of the frozen vegetables all the time to anyone

who'll listen. It just comes out. Sometimes people laugh.
I laugh with them. I was there for my father. Who will be

there for me?

3

This is the season of the tongue, pressed like a dead flower into
a scrap book, lit blue; this is the sleepy time of genocide at

the speed of real estate deals, lit blue; this is the season
of empty snail shells on railroad stones that sing the song

ashes fall, lit blue; this is the time of the contest for the ice-
cream flavor that will save us and capitalism at the same time,

lit blue; this is the time of the image of a locked door, a locked
cage, a locked dumpster, scratched with a nail into the skin, lit

blue: this is the time of the all-seeing eye, watching all
the sleepless souls who have no home hang in the air like

forest fire smoke, lit blue.

4

I keep returning to a set of bear claw scratches I found
scraped across the concrete of an underpass. I try to go

there at least once a week, trace the lines with the tips of
my fingers. The scratches of my own god. Signs of divinity.

Oh yes, I know what father would say: *those gouges are
from a car scraping the cement.* He wasn't addressing me,

he never addressed me. He was always answering some-
thing inside his own head. This world is all scars and

prophecies, if you look close enough. I smear mothwing
dust beneath my eyes, take a deep breath, weave myself

into the dark. I am right here, always right here. Please
look at me.

What Holds Everything Together

1

The Douglas-fir's dead body is not dead. How can it be
dead, half of it still standing, twenty feet into the sky,
trunk five yards in diameter? I place my palm against
the bark, feel the curves of bark beetle galleries beneath,
and the hollow deeper still, the emptiness that holds this
tree together.

2

There are times when I can feel that same emptiness
inside me, the space that stitches together all the parts
of this body—skate-made ripples of pond water, blood
and cortisol, sawdust, marbled meat, and a few red
needles sinking into mud, into the mycelium ley-lines
that hold this entire forest together.

3

What's alive and what's not is unclear here. Listen—
the ecstatic energy of decay, breaking down all bodies
into their source elements. Listen—resurrection is close:
the beat of a heart, shadows moving from tree to tree,
a flurry of dead needles floating down onto dead leaves.
What's alive and what is not is unclear everywhere.

4

I've known this space. Nights in childhood, reaching
out and recoiling from the dark around and inside me.
It has always been here, looking in our windows,
curious, sometimes leaving things under the pillow—
a beetle leg, a pebble of green sea glass, a fish scale
able to reveal the colors hidden inside cold moonlight.

Protozoa, A Cave Painter, A Moth's Tongue:
How the World Was Made

Parasites inside me created and were created by the moon
and now my eyes follow the moon through bare branches.

Protozoa turn my head slowly, so slowly, as if my head
was trying to mimic their ancient blind turning, following

the movements of the moon when the moon walked among
them, spoke with them, performed miracles. They've explained

to us, over and over, how the shadows at the edge of the sea
are our ancestors, how shadows across stone fields are our

ancestors, how shadows deep in the gut are ancestors. When I
finally listened to them, I found myself at the window, studying

orange trumpet flowers where white sphinx moths unfurled
their tongues (Yet another séance held to draw down the moon.

And I was invited to that séance. And you were invited, too.
Insomniacs, we watched a woman pull horses from rock

with charcoal and ochre paste, whispering the thousand names
of the moon, her torch flame leaping and retreating, imitating

the moth's tongue). And I remembered rocking back and forth,
sucking on my own tongue, a sleepless infant, unaware of

the moth's work, flame's tides, but named it for the first time:
Luna. I looked up, saw a woman's face behind glass in

the highest window of the old folk's home next door. What was
she looking at? Horses in moonlight, bounding across the roofs,

putting out the streetlights one by one, returning us to the turning
dark of our intestines, stomachs, liver, lungs, heart.

Ancestors, Early Winter Night

The war continues. The war against grace, breath,
against the bodies of strangely shaped insects,
bark, and manatees with moonscape skin, against
interesting and curious minds; capital dividing and
conquering, leaving so many alone, standing in
silence (the only thing left that's theirs), with an
unbearable ability to hear the last breath of a rabbit
just now tossed from under a car tire, rolling
toward the road's shoulder.

I have so many things to do but can't move. I
stand at the window, headlights sweep across my
face. An image returns: my father passed out on
the kitchen floor, lights blazing at 3 am, Christmas
music playing. I turn off the music, try to pull him
up, but he's too heavy, there are too many bodies
inside his body, weighing him down, so I must talk
him through it, back to his bed. I say the words
calmly, clearly, the way I could not back then. All
of the eyes inside him look into my face. What
do they see?

After putting him to bed, I discovered a street lined
with old sycamores, and began peeling bark, feeling
the acute satisfaction of stripping skin from skin. I
now look down that street in memory and know
those trees as great-grandfathers, great-grandmothers.
Kin. I turn, stare into a dark room, place my hands
into the shadows of those distant trees, searching for
my body, my father's body, for the bodies of those
who cannot help but keep silent vigil beside the dying
and the dead.

Starry Night over the Rhone
(Vincent van Gogh)

Harsh yellow gaslight sent gold ribbons across
the Rhone. I followed those ribbons up into Ursa

Major's seven aquamarine-soft haloes: "seeing" as
spinning out threads of light. Look: the hands,

green stars. Look: the heart, gold gas. I was eight
and I heard him say: *night is richer in color than*

the day. I was eight, and for one second, maybe
two, I knew someone else who sensed night in

the same way. And I reached up, almost touched
the thick paint, and for one second, maybe two,

my muscles were freed from fear, could articulate
how dark and light feed, and are fed. I stood on my

toes and made starlit ripples in the air, mimicked
the feedback loop between my finger bones and

distant star-gas threads. And I saw the couple, almost
in shadow, maybe an after-thought, maybe in love,

at the bottom of the painting, walking back to their
hotel, to get out from under that intense mirror of

their hearts, hands, eyes. And I knew, for one second,
maybe two, that there is no escape, no matter what we

do. Is this memory true? *Night is richer in color than*
the day.

Musée d'Orsay, Paris

Where Do the Bees Go?

1

It's cold, so cold, a wet cold, and the bees
have disappeared into their thin-walled

huts, built out there in the dark somewhere.
They try to sleep in the cold rain, wake,

try sleep again, huddled together in a
bristled crush, breathe as one. Their wing-

vibrations generate a feeble green light,
a light that guides the memories of

the dead back to their source (the image of
a house on fire, eyes glistening in the dark,

a few words like yellowfoot chanterelles
rising from decayed wood or bone).

2

When it's this cold and wet, I stand in
the middle of the room, head-bowed, and

feel the cold as punishment, something
deserved from before birth, and notice

there has always been a slight tremor
beneath my skin, no matter the season.

The bees know why I've always been
cold. Grateful to them, I wonder what I

can leave outside my door tonight that will
let them know I'm thinking of them, that I

believe their dim winter light might help
some part of me find its way back home.

The Hand inside the Pumpkin

A black plastic strip hangs on wire, wind-ragged.
Beyond a controlled fire, pumpkins. Beyond that,
cars and trucks on a straight road.

Dust rises off a field. The column twists. Funnel-
spirits of the dry plowed earth: ancestors, still
twisting with pain, searching for the reflection

of the water-skate's body in black water; for
the bluish-green phosphor lamp of marsh light;
for the salamander dangling, suspended, between

surface and mud floor in a cold pool. When a
door opens between worlds, the skin on the back
of the neck becomes thin, lets in the wind. When

lines become liquid, the hand inside the pumpkin
knocks back. When rain becomes a burning bush,
the mouth that was taught "yes" and "no" dissolves.

There's no rain here. The black plastic strip twists
this way, that; a struggling Houdini. When I was a
child, I was smoke, could slip through keyholes.

A Snake, A Root, A Shoelace:
How the World Was Made

The moccasin created black water in order to move
secretly from one dark world to another. You know this.

I know this, too. This knowledge plays dodge and weave
in the chambers of the heart. It's automatic, so there's no

need to keep time. Systolic. Diastolic. Blood moves
through black water thin with a graceful lazy motion. I

close my eyes and there is the snake's dystopic paradise
of shades, where a black-gum leaf inhales, exhales, on

the black surface, mimics the dying breath of a swamped
rowboat, absence of a rower claimed by the eyes of a

thousand-year-old catfish. Everyone knows those catfish
eyes can blind the sun, dissolve it through a net of dragon-

fly wings. When I remember this, I go blind, too. It's
sympathetic blindness. When I'm blind, the swamp tilts,

hummocks of peat turn inside out, the dead work their
way up through their own corpses to find the snake along

the bank. The snake that is the cypress root. The snake
that is the lace of my untied shoes, no time to tie them,

racing out the door, on a Saturday morning, in flight,
afraid; and the snake is the seam between the shadow-din

of insects never before seen, never named, and the glut-
tonous sun. I make a soft sound, a cry before the first cry,

before tongue and teeth, the cry I made long before I
was named.

Ancestor, At the Edge of Sleep

He lives alone, in a crumbled blue clapboard house,
among a hoard of empty bottles, junk mail, laws,
proclamations and manifestos; a yellowing eugenics
scheme taped to the door of a dead fridge.

I hate him. I fucking hate him.

He can feel this, taunts me, dares me to open my
heart to him. *You know you have to,* he says. It is
a trick. *I was a god,* he says. *I could have fixed it
all . . . someone has to make the hard decisions.*

He's clearly insane. I hate him.

He reminds me that he resides somewhere in my
body. *If I'm insane, you are too.* I can't move
towards him. I cannot leave. He says: *All bodies
in the world used to be mine . . .*

I hate him for drawing me into his story, showing
me his story cannot be separated from mine.

He begs for sympathy. *You don't understand,* he
says, *I made this world. I deserve some respect.* His
world smells of piss, mold, shit. He looks up at me,
red-eyed: *What are you going to do?*

What can I do? I help him stand, lead him slowly
out the door, into the yard. We sit in damp chairs,
side by side, silent. I want him to become entranced
by the leaves above us.

I want him to see the impossibility of separation. I want him to focus so intently on this fusion of light and leaf that he is absorbed back to some beginning place, can start again.

I want, I want, he says, *good god, will you listen to yourself? You sound just like me . . .*

Crossing Western Wyoming
Smothered in Forest Fire Smoke

1

Brown-dust sky, first sky, last sky; smoke descends, settles in, earth
become air. Upside down world, claustrophobic sky, too close to

the car. My brain scans for threat, for strange noises from the engine,
disaster inside disaster—rattles filled with dead flies, distant thuds

of earth collapsing into sudden holes, grunts of extinct animals
echoing off empty missile silo walls.

2

We watch truck lights dissolve in smoke all night from a motel
room sandwiched between a strip club and a drive-in liquor store;

smoke we want to believe will eventually be scoured clean by
wind or sun; while particulate matter weaves deep into the lungs,

into the blood, enters the brain as a dream, watching fire-waves
consume a liquor store roof, and the air above.

3

In the morning, the smoke is thicker. I imagine skeletons out
there, beyond the highway shoulder: hulks of things, like shadows

on a CT scan of the lungs or brain. But during brief moments when
the smoke clears, there is nothing there, all those ruins have moved

back inside me; appear only in how I chew the inside of my lip; in
my shallow, shallow breaths.

Self-Portrait (Rembrandt)

1

Old Man Rembrandt's face looked into mine. In this painting
he is perpetually 63, a year from death. I was 51, death close

from a recent funeral. What did he see? The ones who stopped
in front of the painting and lingered were all older, their faces

lined, slack, beginning that slow decline, like mine; the skin's
longing for earth.

2

Who am I? It used to be a question of failure. *How can you
not know . . . at your age?* We watched each other for an hour.

His face, his eyes, told the story of falling, how light falls, is
revealed by the shadow of deep furrows, thick folds. *Who am*

I? Did he answer that question for himself when he stared
back at this portrait?

3

Staring into his face, I felt my own, how parts were frozen
by fear, fear of everything moving around me, fear of things

that happened long ago, the muscles around my eyes retreating,
wincing, waiting for the blow; but also parts that were more

relaxed, reaching out, listening, curious, wondering *Where is
the end of this thing called I?*

4

On the morning of that recent death, there was a crow on a bridge
rail. A few black feathers lifted and fell in the wind. *Who am*

I? Old Man Rembrandt stared into me, into himself. The crow's
call turned the answer into the question's echo: *Who am I?*

Light falls. Darkness reveals light that is always falling. Down
the hall, in another gallery, someone laughed.

National Gallery, London

Stilling: Red-Tailed Hawk

1

She hovers, wings outstretched.

Tiny-gyres around her extended alula
feathers bind wind to wing.

I am a heartbeat.

2

She hovers, scans for movement;
intuits the distance between beak

and prey. Slight adjustment of her
tail rudder and

I am a breath.

3

She hovers, where Venus appeared
last night.

Inside her stillness, sudden rage rushes
in: so many senseless deaths.

I am what lies between heartbeats.

4

She drops down my spine, disappears
into distant trees.

An empty plastic bottle rolls slightly,
then stills.

I am lichen exploring a nearby oak's
skin.

5

Death, that ancient bird, stilling in
my cells, lies somewhere beneath

this rage. She creates the wind, spins
it, rides it through wing.

I am

Our Mother's Body

1

Her body is the keeper of all secrets. She becomes thinner and thinner, disappearing inside her clothes, trying to become wind. Leaves fly. Walnuts slam against the porch. Winter is almost here.

Her body believes in national security, has the burden of keeping the things that should not be said from being said, keeping the things that should not be felt from being felt, keeping the things that should not be remembered from being remembered.

Night after night, when I look in the mirror I see her drunk father stumble into the house, stare through her, leaving the door ajar. Snow blows across the floorboards. I see our mother's mother stare out the kitchen window, transparent, silent, and thin, so thin, also disappearing.

Our mother's mother whispers about the bells that rang for the dead in 1347, 1665, 1899 . . . Her brothers and sisters died in 1918, leaving her alone with mute parents and a dog. Someone saw her walking the dog and wanted to put her in the movies. She is now in a movie taking place inside our mother's body. In the movie, she counts the dead by her repetition of the word "bells."

Encrypted messages pass back and forth between satellites that shoot across the night sky, so far above the earth. I stare at my face in the mirror, cannot look at my body. I know parts of my body are starting to disappear, too. I don't know how to bring anything back.

2

The snow outside is sparse, becomes rain. The Enola Gay
lifts off the tarmac inside our mother's body, sails into an
elevator shaft that takes a group of officers to a lead-encased
office beneath the earth where they plan World War III.
Someone must do it. If they don't do it, then the wrong kind
of people will do it. We're locked into this pattern. This is
just how the economy works.

Rain falls onto wet snow. The grey roofs seen from this
window merge with the grey sky. Inside our mother's body
the officers draw a mushroom cloud, calculating the circum-
ference of the blast, checking it against population stats. Our
mother believes they are making this sacrifice beneath the
earth in order to redeem the world from its own frightening
emptiness.

No matter their sacrifice, our mother hears it. The emptiness
whispers to her; hand, mouth, breast, hip, thigh and face that
can never be found, exists in everything she touches. She
stands, suspended in the middle of a thought. She remembers
something, opens a cabinet, looks in. No, not that.

A skinless figure appears, looks at her through the kitchen win-
dow. The kitchen light glints off the crown of its flayed head.
Its long fingernails scratch at glass, longing to get inside, touch
her.

I know this figure. It appears in my dreams: waiting in a dark
doorway. It follows me into the subway. Sometimes I believe
it caught up to me years ago. Maybe I am already dead. Maybe
I was reborn as a stone, just now rising to the surface of a bare
field after a spring thaw, four hundred miles north.

3

Our mother walks down a tree lined path, grips my arm with one hand, holds an instamatic with the other. She carries the camera with her whenever she leaves the house.

By late childhood, I shied from her touch. This time, I feel something deeper than memory—the bones below. Solidity. Roots and stones. I have a flash of walking the path, both of us skeletons, post-death, enjoying the park, slowly becoming water, bark.

If photos are taken, they are never of her. That is taboo. She hates photos of herself. But this time I say, "How about I take a picture of you?" For the first time in my life she smiles, sheepish, and says okay.

In the photo our mother stands in front of a pond, arms stiff at her sides, eager to please, to look good, a child posing for a school photo, even though she is now a child of bones.

Holding the photo, I feel my own finger bones, my spine, my skull, the muscles and tendons wrapped around the bones.

The Rest of the Body

1

The swash moves fast, out of shoaling waves, chases
us toward cedar cliffs, drowning fresh-water rivulets,

like a foam-headed creature ignorant of its power,
playing tag. It rushes down worm holes, flushing

plankton and fish scraps into ravenous open mouths,
linking the worms back to the sea, to the rest of their

body. A part of me wants to stop, turn, let myself be
absorbed, worm-grateful, while the rest of me keeps

running up the beach until the wave finds the limits
of its reach.

2

You find an empty mussel shell. The inside reveals
light pulled inside out, iridescent, the glee of a

spectrum change with each new angle; the place
where light was trapped (or made?) inside the shell,

folded in by tidal rhythm, frayed particles of marine-
snow drift, and the motion of a thousand tail fins.

Small bits of flesh still cling to the shell's hinge,
right below that dazzling color-shift. We laugh,

suddenly linked back to the rest of the body, parts
we didn't know we'd missed.

Refugee

Our findings suggest that warming-induced body
size reduction is a general response to climate change
and reveal a similarly consistent and unexpected
shift in body shape. We hypothesise that increasing
wing length represents a compensatory adaptation to
maintain migration as reductions in body size have
increased the metabolic cost of flight.
—Ecology Letters 2020

Circles pass through each other on the pond's surface,
envelop a child's cry.

Turkey vultures enter the sun, exit through its burning
back door, into the noise of a nearby highway.

How do the vultures contain Death's anger, Death's
melancholy, Death's desperate desire to merge?

When will vulture bodies get too small to shelter all of
Death's needs, that haunted longing?

Refugee, it will roam from one body to another—blue-
gills, tarsiers, dragonflies, human bodies—testing . . .

Can I sustain that cold kiss to the heart, the eye? Circles
intersect, envelop my cold silence.

Vulture wings glide over water, luxurious, hold up
the sun's light, lend shade to the dying and the dead.

Glaze Event: How the World Was Made

The ice-storm created the trees, the cars, the crows on
the boulevard, by encasing them in ice; gave glistening

birth to roofs, chimneys, doors, dead dogs, scattered
garbage, stray furniture abandoned on sidewalks. Ice

was the temperature of my room after the transmission
towers sent an arc of white light across the sky and

everything went dark. All night, I kept candle-lit vigil
with the ash outside the window, watching it bend low,

lower, under the greyweight of ice wrapped around ice.
All night: explosions, when other trees cracked in half,

crashed through phone wires, onto the icy street. Come
morning, the ash was still whole, and to celebrate (and

stay warm) I went out to explore. No sound, no sound,
for miles, for hours, until I heard *shk-shk shk-shk,*

shk-shk shk-shk: a girl, 11 or 12, skating down the center
line of the boulevard, one fist swinging with the rhythm

of her skates, the other pressed to the small of her back.
(I was encased there in that sound, the only sound. You

were encased there, too. And now we hold constant vigil
over the loss of ice—it's beauty, danger, it's agonized

mythology: a storm of ice needles birthed from the death-
throes of a lone sunflower stalk that grew through the eye

socket of an antelope skull out on the great plains . . .) And
she passed—*shk-shk shk-shk*—as if she was the last ghostly

word from the storm. Or the first of one yet to come.

Ancestors, Out There

1

I feel them when I pass light from a distant
farm window, far off the highway in Nebraska
or Northeastern Colorado, or when I see a

distant streetlight over an empty crossroad. A
few snowflakes drift through the light, land
somewhere in the dark. Or never land at all.

2

Cold stares from sepia faces, face muscles tense
for the long exposure. Weddings, funerals;
enduring their life for some promised future, lost

to the place they left, parts of their bodies never
able to land here, and so always angry, seething
in the dark: ghosts roaming inside ghosts.

3

I see them at the corner of my eyes, standing in
frozen mud-furrows, crouching in the snow on an
overpass embankment, hiding under dried corn

leaves. Why can't they move on? Because of
the future. *Future*, a holy word for them. It still is.
It keeps them moving, still moving, never still.

4

Welcome to the future, I say, inside this car with
no heater, a hole rusted through the floor of
the passenger well. I stop the car on the shoulder,

get out, stand in the cold. One of them steps out
of the dark, hands me a wood carving of a deer—
or an elk: a creature between there and here.

5

The carving has intricate branching antlers. Roots
search the sky, press into my hand, and I suddenly
explode across the snow-drifted plain. During

the long night of running, of leaping, I look down,
see my antlered shadow cross the moon's reflection
in ice. *Who are we? Who are we, really?*

6

I get back in the car, continue west. Ten miles
down the road, I stop again, offer the carver
my loneliness, the loneliness of a hawk perched

high in a lone cottonwood, half-asleep, snow on
his wings, waiting for dawn, a world of new snow;
the loneliness I probably inherited from him.

7

I travel through a sea of snow dust, boulders, figures
who shift and change all night long. The road is so
close, heard through the hole in the floor. Like breath

on the back of my neck from a creature who's been
hunting me all night. The farm light disappears over
the edge of the earth.

Nacer de Nuevo/Rebirth (Remedios Varo)

She pushes through matted roots, emerges into an earthen room,
sees the root-sprouted table that holds a water-filled grail. She

emerges, lit from within, from the sun inside the earth. Call her
Luminar. In the middle of a busy bookstore, I recognized that

image though I'd never seen it before. How did she know what
had been inside me since birth? A hole in the root-ceiling revealed

a crescent moon, reflected off the water's surface. She stares into
the reflection, entranced, pleased, at the threshold of the room she

has been searching for her entire life, but hadn't known existed
until that moment. Call her *Liminar*. And I stood there, looking

down at that painting, *Luminar* as *Liminar*, entranced, perpetually
breaking through, into the secret; rooted to a room moving in and

out of time. I was the chalice bearing the moon's illusive tracks;
the woman hatched into the root-room, discoverer and discovered

at the same time; the slim arched door beyond the table holding
the grail, opening out to distant bare trees, night trees, keeping

silent vigil. So many selves suddenly available. Now, every time
I look at this painting, she says to me: *We are not just one thing,*

never just one thing. I take in a deep breath, my first breath...

*Painting first seen in "Women Artists and
the Surrealist Movement" by Whitney Chadwick*

Low

The blue heron flew wing-shadow low across my chest
and my blue hunger was pulled into its wake, into
the black stones at my feet that surfaced to meet her cross.

Orange-green lichen settled into the scar left by her cry;
and I followed those spiraled paths over roots, traversed
low-slung web funnels, into the undergrowth.

Is this my return home or am I crawling into a place I've
never been? The low smell remains the same: brown
worm mung and blue vine-twist (both balm and sting).

There's also the smell of forest smoke. Brown sky. Low
sun, fire-red, absorbing ash, absorbing rage, trying to
beat back sorrow . . .

I see her crouched low. She stabs the water, swallows
all bodies she's ever been—two-legged theropod,
revealed in the speed of each yellow eye.

Nerve-arc lit, connects her to an end, a beginning, bird
to lizard to spine lightning, eye to fish, wraps Time
itself, that low heartbreak of slow change.

And this slowly-evolved heart, how can it keep pace
with all that disappears from the earth each night? Pain
pools in low places, an invasion of shades.

I emerge at the water's edge. Low reflection of her
silhouette high in a dead oak. I kneel. A nutria's rat-
tail cuts between clusters of floating yellow-heart . . .

Car Batteries, Falling Snow, Snakestones

1

Snow flies in from the south in waves; thick with huge flakes, then
sparse, with flakes so small they float, can't make it to earth. Cars

slice through grey snow on Coburg Road, most heading to work. I
can't. Someone stole my car battery last night. No damage, though.

Were they purposefully careful? But why bother? Maybe this is
the new way we look out for each other . . .

2

I weave my hands in an ascending spiral through falling flakes, long
for a world where, when the snow falls, everything we call 'normal

life' stops, leaves us still, watching the flakes fall, eyes empty as an
echo off a cave wall, hands resolute as a hawk scanning a field of

snow, hearts that mimic a family of sour-smelling mice curled together
beneath roots and ice, spacious as the journey of every stone.

3

Footprints follow me through wet snow. I crouch down, study
the prints and laugh, recognize them as ones I've been tracking

for decades, since birth. In my pocket there's a black ammonite,
a fossil that looks like a coiled snake without a head; a mollusk at

least 66 million years dead: I run my fingers along the frilled suture
lines. The only clock I know that tells the true time.

Something Inside (Dreadful Euphoria)

We hide behind a dune. Sand scours sand up the smooth slope.
Sand in the eyes, ears; sand through the mind. I think about being
buried alive and laugh.

I have something inside me.

A bank of mist on the horizon looks like a tsunami wall, and I
think about the relief that will come when I'm torn apart in that
wave and laugh.

I have something inside me.

Mist floats over us. Thin shadow-ribbons move up the dunes,
across our faces. Gulls snatch empty crab shells from each other.
Shadows of things to come, of things past. I laugh.

I have something inside me.

What is this half-formed creature inside, yearning, desperate, all
mouth, hungry, that I have beaten back into the dark for so long,
denied exists, that craves an all-encompassing end?

I have something inside.

I reach out and touch that dark half-life, made of street mucous,
melted plastic Christmas wreaths, and the particulate matter lifted
from the souls of burning trees and slaughtered pigs.

I have something.

Inside Leonora Carrington's Painting *The Giantess* While Standing at the Edge of a Pond

1

Moon-faced, wheatfield hair, she stares past my right shoulder,
into herself, the world, right here, at the edge of the water, where

geese fly from her white cape. Their wings beat air, stir it into
Miocene words telepathically passed between the bird-people

embroidered on her red dress, questioning each other; questioning
me, questioning you: *What is the name of the child who was able*

to name each individual bee that ever lived? Can you summarize
the geological plot hidden inside the narrative of a feathered

snake's eye?

2

She is holding an egg. The egg contains the body of this world,
where herons nest in high bare branches, their necks secret

feathered snakes that fold in on themselves when no one is looking;
gold eyes that survey the land below, leaving a gold brand on

everything they notice. There's a gold imprint on my forehead
that burns. I reach up, touch it and am back in the painting, in

the egg that is her body towering over tiny villagers chasing an
amphibious, winged tree-spirit, hunting their origins, not knowing

what they will do if they ever catch up. Maybe the youngest among
them will ask the right question: *What is the color of mercy when*

the moons of Neptune stop conversing? Can you calculate the root
of the root of the word mycorrhiza?

3

The blue whale in the sea behind her blows a fish-weed scented
spray that illuminates a woman in a boat, arms spread, warning off

harpooners, while ghostly sea creatures of every shape emerge and
disappear beneath the pond's surface. Ghost crabs, ghost manta

rays, ghost sea-insects flown in by giant geese from Proteus churn
the water unnoticed, feed on each other unnoticed. *Go back, go*

back, stay on land, she says, until you can feel these invisible threads
between manta ray and geese, whale and wheat, moon and egg,

painting and pond. Go back, before it's too late.

4

But it's always too late. I have always been inside this painting,
this egg, inside this towering body that conjures gravity for spinning

geese birthed into a skein-mantra formation that is the world, that is
the cliff threshold between land and sea, that is eight turtles side by

side on a half-submerged fallen tree mid-pond, all heads stretched
toward the sky, staring up into geese shadows, ectomycorrhizal

cloud-threads forming a mantle around the earth, around so many
questions: *How long will the last blue whale's song sail through*

the ocean? Will it break the bodies of those who can still hear?
Who is asking this question?

Delta Ponds, Eugene, Oregon

What's Not There Calls to Me

What's not there calls to me. Can you hear it? Wind over an
empty bottle half-buried in sand, edge of the high-tide line.

Spray lifts off foam, becomes a seagull, becomes a grey veil.
I sometimes make lists of things that have replaced what's no

longer there: *microplastics, iphones, 3d printers, blockchains,
ghost nets* . . . words that developed too quickly to have roots.

They hover just above me, their cameras send images of this
poem back to a bunker full of server racks, in a secret location

beneath the earth, where green and red lights illuminate specks
of dust. What's not there keeps calling out to me. Do I mistake

it for the odd distant voices produced by tinnitus? Is that all it
really is? I want to know that the calls from what's not there are

separate from my own small wounds. A gull lands nearby, eyes
me, searching for something I don't have. I ask the gull if it hears

what's no longer there, too. *Sometimes,* it says, *inside an empty
crab shell.* I laugh—good joke—then open my wings, flap twice,

lift off sand, and sail into the fog blowing in off the water.

Snow Clouds, Space, and Snow-Ghosts: How the World Was Made

The western buttes spun snow clouds out of their last
skeletal memories, dark grey, and sent them east.

After an hour, flakes landed on pitted black volcanic
rock and quickly dissolved, as if they'd never been.

Who will remember them? Who will tell their story
from birth to death and resurrection? Unable to move,

our eyes and fingers became crystal, grey patterns of
ice and space. Flakes drifted out over the gorge, and

we watched as some caught a rising current, ascended
back to their origin, the way some of us do at birth,

opening our eyes into this new world, so stunned by
the light and noise, we rush back into the darkness, to

tell the shadows that had been our family for thousands
of years what we've seen and heard. I keep looking for

that snow, that space between flakes, that thought-
dissolving silence—under rocks, between furrows of

bark, in mist, tufts of dry grass, in the mirror. You keep
looking for it, too. We look for it together in our own

way, grey-eyed children of snow, of the ghosts of snow,
slowly becoming snow-ghosts ourselves, shadows that

appear at the corner of the eye. I can see the last person
to witness sparse snow fall into the gorge, suddenly

blessed and cursed with knowing—for a few seconds—
snow's story, its history of water, dust, condensation,

of ice, dissolution and silence; blessed and cursed with
knowing how deeply snow's memory is entangled with

ours. Will they be reduced to eating cinders, ash, from
grief? And will they then carry that story within them,

in the way they touch another's face? So light, so light,
leaving behind only what is needed in that moment,

barely a trace . . .

Ancestors, Day of the Dead

Sage-smoke weaves around yellow leaves,
wraps a bare, black trunk. I hear the heat-
crack of hollow stems and you appear out

of the smoke. I say: so many of us have lost
our way. I say: it's complicated, and yet there's
still a need to blame. I say: I want to return to

that dimly lit kitchen again, watch your hands
knead dough, while you tell a story about some-
one in the family when they were young.

(But this is not you as I once knew you. This
is you as you are now: half-smoke, vague guide,
weaving something new). I was in that kitchen

so rarely, always passing through. Years after
your death I found your notes in an old copy
of *Labyrinth of Solitude*. Incomprehensible

scrawl, written after you were almost blind.
I thought: odd, so uncharacteristic, to be reading
that book. I didn't know you at all, not really.

(But this is not you as I once believed I knew
you. This is you as you are now: half-smoke,
vague guide, weaving something new). I

thought if I could decipher those words, I
would have a key, some key, *the* key . . . And
I hear you say (this new you, this smoke-

figure): if there's a key, where would the door
be? Please tell me a story tonight, whoever you
are. I promise I will follow you, ride the flying

elm leaves over the street, go wherever you
lead. Tell me a story that links the family back
to the first human face, a story about how we

emerged from the mouth of night, smoking.
Include love and fire. Don't forget horror and
water. Or agony and earth, beauty and air.

Beauty and air and smoke. (I don't care if it's
not you, I still want you to thread this world
together, so I can emerge as a dry leaf, a

burning leaf, a crack from the heated space
inside a hollow stem . . .)

Sounding: How the World Was Made

Sea lions sound the cave walls, sound the waves beating against
the cave entrance, sound the fissures and holes the waves make,

shaped like Silurian fish heads and predator worms. Sea lion
barking echoes off the sea-soaked lichen woven into stone, loud

enough to flay mind from muscle, muscle from bone; a sound
that forces me to suck in the sea-stink of their breath; each drop

of spray a cacophony of bacteria releasing dimethyl sulphide
from sounding dead phytoplankton. Iodine air, algae air, dead

fish-belly scent, brings the bilateral shape of my body into being,
brings the bilateral shape of your body into being, too. Our bodies,

an echo of that first sea worm with mouth and shithole: to shout
joy at the sea along with the sea lions, making a map of the sea-

depths and ourselves at the same time; and then dump our waste
into the waves—create vast plastic-infested gyres, spinning,

deathless, where coastal anemones and brittle stars still cling, far
from home; feeling the map of it all, where each body senses

euphoria (whatever euphoria means to that particular shape); and
each body is also a hole, an absence, a loss, an echo of loss.

Two Turkey Vultures: Early Spring

1

Light rain through new leaves. Two red lizard
heads turned, scanned us. Their spectral eyes

revealed the movement of my own blood to me,
all the minute threads that connect thigh to heart

to throat; revealed the sensation of my bones
exposed to wind, rain; revealed that I have been

waiting for her death for years and now that it is
finally near, the knowledge that I'm not ready,

have never been ready, because *being ready* is
not death's concern.

2

They opened black wings, flew across the river,
over pink bloom, purple petals, mud-tinted foam

folding around the branches of submerged trees,
fertilizing the vortex of ecstatic colors and motion

with the shiver of death. And those bodies revealed
to me that she also possessed black wings, a hooked

beak, a taste for carrion, but had never known, and
that because this was her inheritance, it was mine,

too; and that there is no origin, no beginning place
for how this came to be.

3

After she dies, the seas will begin their slow boil,
under burnt-orange skies, sun filtered through

smoke, a sick-light illuminating our faces, and her
death will remind me what her broken body and

mind passed on to me: that I have these wings,
this hooked beak, stomach acid that burns disease-

carrying bacteria clean. Walking back to the car,
there was a long black vulture feather someone

had stuck into an empty rivet hole in a steel street
light pole. It pointed the way.

Bees, Faeries, Souls of the Dead, Maitake Mushrooms: How the World Was Made

When I was five, I was swarmed by bees; a blanket of bee bodies
covered my head, torso; bee bodies searched up my nose, circled

the roof of my mouth, spoke to each other inside my ears. I am
perpetually caught between the terror of anticipating a thousand

stings and relief from feeling such closeness, the weight of all
those bodies who had chosen *me*, chosen to touch *me*, cover me,

in a way that human beings, up to that time, had not. I still feel
the brush of wings and leg-tines against my skin on the edge of

sleep. For weeks afterwards, late at night, I saw small figures
with transparent wings spiral around the spindly apple tree in our

tiny backyard, each one able to generate their own wan blue glow,
as if they had swallowed a sliver of starlight that had been hiding

deep inside sandstone since the Cambrian explosion of life. For
years I believed faeries were the shape bees take when they sleep

and dream. Sometimes I think they were the souls of dead bees
who had foreknowledge of all future pollinators, trying to digest

and decompose their fate, before all the various plagues settled
in. No answers, then or now. I still see them. I believe you do,

too. Through mist after a night rain, in the ethereal almost-light
beneath damp oaks, conjured from water, sorrow, invisible spores.

When we move slowly towards that light at dawn, sometimes we
find clusters of small spoon-shaped gill-less maitake mushroom

caps, yet another shape the dead take, sending us endless messages
from the underworld.

Watching Apricot Blossoms Fly
during a Time of Plague

Second week of lockdown, no sound in the canyon.
Stones and beetles keep to themselves. Ravens call

to each other, dark jokes about human fear: *Rub*
onions or a sliced snake on your skin. Eat arsenic,

drink mercury, or pour bleach into your eyes (so
you can't see what's ahead). Oval apricot petals

glide over the roof, a flurry of pink against blue. I
follow one petal, track the pattern of its flight, feel

a strange euphoria as my insides lift with the falling.
Seven months later, I am lying in bed, unable to

move, caught in a fever dream: *look! here's a dirty*
old plague doctor with a huge papier-mâché nose,

leering at a young girl, alone, locked in a tiger cage.
He leans in with his white coat, a pair of steel balls

roll in his palm . . . click, click . . . Brain broken, I
welcome the end the way the raven's cry welcomes

families and their things tossed onto the street,
welcomes dead bodies crushed against the harsh

road. Icicles melt outside, drops hit the window
ledge . . . *click, click . . .* Shaking with chills, I hear

voices outside, from the patio below, talking
about fake this, fake that. *No virus. Hoax. No*

global warming, look at this snow . . . The strange
euphoria just before the fall. We can't touch or be

in close proximity to each other and so we can't
hide from each other anymore. Oh god, I desperately

need a poem that falls with the truth of rain falling
on a freshly cut trench filled with body bags. I hear

my own mocking laughter, mimicking the ravens,
remembering the blossoms last spring. Did those

petals find their way to the sun's palace, or to
underworld root-tunnels, riding black water with

the forgetful dead? But all that came later, was only
a shadow in a corner of the eye: the hallucinations,

the depression, the insomnia, the long recovery (I
still can't smell and taste things right: *fake smells,*

fake tastes) But right now, here, the petals have
fallen and the sun is beginning to set. Shadow-chill

on the skin. I suddenly hear a cricket that has probably
been scraping his song all day. He guides one star,

two stars, a hundred stars, into the night sky.

Dragonfly in the Palm

"The Eros of reality begins with touch.
There is no life without contact. Without touch,
there is no desire, no fulfillment—and no mind."
—*Matter and Desire: An Erotic Ecology,* Andreas Weber

1

It's cool. The chitinous exoskeleton guards a soft
middle: heart and nerve cord that connect thoracic
muscles to wing, wing to water, water-shadow to
the sun's reflection on water, sun's reflection on
water to the center of my palm.

2

My skin is azure, my hand floats inside the sky. I
am a sudden peasant child in 12th century Iceland,
just stumbled upon a North African Vagrant
Emperor blown off-course. An insect never seen
before on this island, emissary of some distant
voracious god, maybe the god itself. Its greenish-
yellow compound eyes rove across my face, divine
thirty different pigments, dowse for the secrets
those colors possess, secrets no other human has
ever seen, will ever see.

3

Listen: I lived old age first, breathed through gills
in my rectum, ate bloodworms, mosquito larvae;
then, after one of earth's eons, climbed a stalk,
split my skin into wings. The final stage I lived
as a child, shimmering; water's prophet to
the world of air; fire's excited prophet to earth.
When it was time to die, I flew into the sun, ate
sunlight, returned as light on water.

The god in my palm sees the blue vapor of
sorrow rise from a scorched ponderosa pine;
sees the magenta particles of hunger cling to
a line of ants dismantling a rabbit corpse; sees
the shimmering clouds of cerulean blue and
celadon green from that holy and desperate
desire to live escaping from an abandoned
truck trailer; sees the earth-yellow aura of
loneliness around a girl waiting for a mother
who will never arrive; sees the amethyst violet
of gravity, endlessly drawing everything
together.

5

It lifts off, circles me, moves backwards,
forwards, an intricately complicated diagram
where sky, mandible, palm, joy, death, tarsus
and hunger meet. I feel a hole in the center of
my palm, as if my hand had been formed from
this dragonfly's need for a landing space
three hundred million years ago, and its
purpose is suddenly gone—leaving a prophecy
of mosquito clouds, the size of small cities,
feasting on the sun.

6

I am the architect of air, architect of sun, arch-
itect of sun on water, of water-shadows eating
water-shades beneath your hand dangling in
dark pond water; architect of the water's
surface continually breaking the sun into its
elemental colors, colors beyond your abilities
to see, but know are there, ghosts moving
close, just out of reach, a question that never

quite forms in the brain; breaking you into
your elemental parts: one part mosquito in
the beak of a cedar waxwing, one part green
wave foam slipping across wet sand, one part
charcoal, and one part sunlight burrowing into
leaf veins in the space between waves of rain;
a recipe I coded into the genes.

7

I could hear it, hear it but not see it, hear
several other dragonflies out there, spinning
around each other. Listen: somewhere inside
that sound, a hydrogen moon moves through
the chambers of my heart. Listen: somewhere
inside the sound, the source of the spiral
shaped snail shell inside my inner ear. Listen:
wind and a lemon balm stem have joined
together, formed the solidity beneath my
feet. Listen: this is how my body sounds in
the aftermath. Listen: the dragonflies are
still out there, moving in and out of
existence.

Blue Pool at Tamolitch Falls

1

Down the cliffside, it's azure-clear, too clear, color
that may be the origin of water itself; and turquoise-
cold, so cold nothing can live down there.

Fall into the illusion: reflection and depth merge. Old
growth trees, thirty feet down, seem only a few yards
below the surface.

Can the illusion answer the question posed by our
first desperate breath, memory hidden inside the rise
and fall of the chest?

2

There's a silence down there. It pulls at me, as if
I'm in the wake of death wings making their rounds
at twilight beneath the tree canopy.

When the skies begin to boil, the trees flame to ash,
and this pool is sucked into the sky, becomes a circle
of baked mud cracks, that silence will remain,

inside a shell of dried clay, waiting for the promised
huge sand-colored insects, who will carry it with them,
grain by grain, into the next world.

The Autumn People

1

I catch the orange glow of their cigarettes out beyond
the tracks in late Fall: all those we've killed in so many

of our wars, those caught in our furious crossfire, our
vicious metallic arguments with ourselves. I hear them

pad down to the river at night with zinc buckets to get
water for coffee, to keep them awake, vigilant. They

may be dead but they are still wary of us. Each footfall
is soft as the shift of a fin below the river's surface.

2

They have been gathering their forces, waiting patiently
until they have enough mass to rush the city, shut down

the grid, the water, stop traffic, grind the tired economy
to a halt, eliminate sleep. (Maybe it's already happened:

Insomnia has built a strong following here.) Sometimes
they steal into the city in twos and threes, rummage

recycling bins, clink glass jars together to find the perfect
sound that will bring all the walls and bridges down.

3

They have a saying they pass on to the newly dead in their
camps. I hear it lying awake at night: *everything is happening*

at once. I can feel it's truth. Everything *is* happening at once.
There are moments when I believe they have already stormed

the city, that it's already over. Last night on my rounds I passed
a body sleeping (or dead) beneath a thin blanket. The wind

lifted the frayed corner. I saw a hand, relaxed. Me, I welcome
the invasion, a revelation of secrets the dead will reveal.

4

This morning, impatient, I went out to them, crossed the tracks,
waded through high grass, into the line of trees beside the river,

to tell them that it's time, everything's cracking and breaking
apart of its own accord, and it may only take a breath, a whisper,

a nudge, to shut everything down, start anew. On a mud bank,
I found two men, talking over each other, full of rapid-fire

meth-inspired words, focused on how to fix a bike so they
could sell it, the fantastic things they would do with the cash . . .

Moth Hovering between
Two Incense Cedars

Hatched early by a warm February,
it floated above us, flicker of beige
wings, harmonics of dust: stone-shift

crushing together snow landing on
brown fur, flip of an ear against a
cloud of flies, sun reflected off trans-

parent wings, tongue that washes its
own eye, spine cold as lightning, an-
tennae folded inside a night-wrapped

cocoon, brush of fin against red sea-
leaf, blood-crust on a black hoof, into
an intricate veined pattern; ladders

and labyrinths of dust containing
what's extinct mingled with what's
not yet found its shape, dust to dust-

wings to dust again. And then it was
gone, as if it had disappeared into a
fold in space made by cedar branch

shadows; this brief glimpse of dust-
light by dust-eyes, as we dissolved
into spore and moon's breath; passed

through cedar bark; slight vibrations,
almost as if we'd never been.

Jésus-Christ Nous Offrant Son Sang
(Gustave van de Woestyne)

1

The god of death is always with us, constant companion, hanging off his cross with his crown of thorns, brushing against our skin, staring at us through red-rimmed, bugged out, bloodshot eyes, always curious, wondering if we have felt it yet, that sudden shock of being alive, the lucid-ache of *I am here*. Inside that intense stare is kindness, a non-human kindness, the same kindness found down along the banks of the Willamette River just now, between the wind and black cottonwood leaves.

2

There are two, positioned at the bottom of the cross, at the bottom of the painting. A Mary figure, in a nun's habit; and a blonde child, pale, orphaned by some twentieth century war massacre, asked to stand beneath this cross, hold her hands in the same bowl-shape the nun makes—but the girl's sorrow is focused on something else, something beyond the body on the cross, something she knows will always be moving through her body, shape her story until the day of her death. And the god looks out of the painting at me, as if to say *You see . . . You see how it is . . .*

3

This god knows our death, the one born with us, that grows with us, our doppelganger, invisible twin. Mary looks like a silent film star expressing horror and hope at the same time, as if the god's gaze has ignited the death waiting inside her, given her access to its knowledge. The god keeps looking out at me, dares me to believe that we have the right to experience all of our emotions, to experience them any way we can, sometimes tied together in a confusing knot all at once, and so know that ecstatic lament *I am here*.

4

Years go by without me looking at this painting, forgetting it's printed on a postcard trapped inside some box in the closet. I pull it out, half-expecting that the god will have disappeared from the painting while I wasn't looking, leaving Mary and the girl and me alone, to continue the story of our grief, so that when the face of our death reveals itself to us, we will reach out, touch its cheek. Out the window, cottonseed from black cottonwood trees that line the riverbanks south of here float through a grey sky—snow on a cool spring twilight.

Musées Royaux des beaux-arts de Belgique, Bruxelles

Stone Shrieks, Birthday Balloons, Wind Sickness: How the World Was Made

Wind-dry, five months straight, another forever to go. High
desert spring winds year-round now. Dust works its way

through these window seams, seams in my brain; glass on
constant rattle; bent-back cry of the locust outside. Leaves

fly mid-summer, twisted from shriveled stems. Wind instead
of water, instead of earth; wind to feed the fire, the shriek of air

into air, trying to escape into itself, wind-fist against the door:
please let me in, please, something is out here, let me in. I felt

the wind-sickness hollow out my bones. I know you felt
it, too. I saw it in your face, turned to a whispering screen,

tuned to the voices worming their way into the heart. *This will
go on forever. There is no hope.* I saw a balloon, a helium-

filled birthday balloon, shining against the fierce sun, sailing
northeast over town. And I heard the wind say that I could go,

too, like the balloon, float to the wind's palace, offered final
asylum; safe from the voices, the constant scouring of lizard

skin and stone, from all these wind-sick seizures and shrieks.
Have some peace. *Peace.* Where I can move from cool room

to cool room, communing with all those who died in claustro-
phobic heat-stroked rooms, mouths gratefully open to flying

dust, believing the sound of the wind against the world was
water, falling.

The Disappeared

1

Bodies have been disappearing on this street for weeks.
Shadows grow longer at the edge of streetlight. I feel

them, out there, being handed off on airport tarmacs,
picked up on the road's shoulder, instantly becoming

faceless, anonymous bodies with nervous systems.
Nerves that will become extensions of wires that lead

to the soft fingers and mouths of interrogators who do
not seek answers, never answers, only pain.

2

I look down into the Willamette River: headlights pierce
each other behind me. There are wires beneath this

river, snaking out across the globe, attaching themselves
to bodies, stolen bodies. Follow the strands and you move

toward the world's central secret. I hate secrets, but I
hoard them just the same. I've seen the bodies float down

the river in the dark. I've seen the interrogator's claws
reach up, pull the bodies down. I say nothing.

3

What is the primary drug for those who keep busy
designing ways to torture; the primary drug of those

who carry it out, tinkering with knobs, dials? Is it
the same drug taken by those who are in charge of

nuclear silos? Living on top of power so vast and secret
it must suck all life out of everything around it, create

a life of its own. There is an occult power in torture,
secrets, the ability to disappear bodies.

4

What is the body? Vulnerable meat marbled by threads
of light, reaching out for and retreating from pain. I

move quickly, at the speed of thought, try to keep from
being completely solid, remain only mind. If I'm not a

solid body that can sense, can be attached to the intricate
web of wires that are endlessly searching for nerve-endings,

I will no longer be desirable to them. I grow long, with
shadows at the end of the street, evade detection.

Reprieve

The red eye of the spotted towhee, the red eye of the spotted,
and the black pupil, the black pupil wrapped by red ionized

hydrogen gas clouds, the red eye, the red eye of the spotted
towhee, black center spinning, drawing in my chronic fear,

fear of the end, the end of all that surrounds me right now –
orange and black feathers, the sylph-shine of rain drops

hung from small red maple leaves, the towhee's trill phrase
calling the rain down, into my palms, my eyes—all of it

dissolving; this fear of mass extinction, that slow black mass
that follows us close, so close, right behind, over the shoulder,

keeping me moving fast, faster, to get away, some part of
me believing a temporary death sentence reprieve will arrive

from some unknown secret person or place. *It can't really
end, can it?* My fear of the end circles with the churning gas

at the border between red and black in the eye, the eye of
the spotted, border where light begins its trick, bent to black,

disappearing into some underside-of-light whirlpool, that
unknown black hole embrace. But the red inside the eye,

inside the eye of, piercing and wary, tosses my fear back,
fear-particles thrown out, scattered, before they enter the pupil,

into the leaves of a nearby oak. Another illusion. Another
illusion of reprieve. For one more day, one more month, one

more year . . . *just one more, please . . .*

Mourning

1

Midnight, waiting for snow. It's so quiet I hear you—
across a continent, across time—pour wine into your
mug, drink, hear your dark incantations, whispered words
given to you by the hungry ancestors that crowd your
body, trying to exorcise words given to them. *Who would
love you? Shut up! You are worthless. Shut up!*

2

It's so still I can make out the dark words you scribbled
across so many notes, torn pieces crowding the space
beneath your bed; angry, accusatory, words driven like
nails through your bedroom wall by the handless stumps
of your beloved and hated ancestors, hiding behind plaster-
board. *Who would love you? Shut up! Please shut up!*

3

The first flakes begin to fly, they touch stone, glass, singe
warmth from the world. *Who would love you?* I hear a
voice in my head repeat those dark words. They rise from
the borderland between sleep and frost, incomprehensible,
white crystal ice weaving a pattern through my skin. *Shut up!*

4

Snow in my hair, in my hands. Did you ever wake, hear
the snow touch glass, realize you only have this one life,
that this is all there is? No matter the pain poured into our
bodies by others, it's still our only life. *Shut up ... please
shut up ...*

Oracular Melodies

Sitting on oak roots, I watch an ambulance pull
out of the hospice parking lot. Headlights cross

my eyes. No siren. Silence the signal a dead body
is passing. Head against bark, I hear the oak's

music, the way I did as a child: how light taps
leaf, wakes slithering shadows inside the trunk;

perpetual newborns, their voices puncture air with
a-rhythmical hisses, invite the underworld to rise

and join in (don't call hearing this music a wound
... some dark auditory hallucination from a beating,

neglect, or fear of death ...). I can hear the oracular
melody of the stone next to my foot, resting against

a root: the sustained pitch of distant flies on a car-
cass, a drone-chorus that revels in and laments death

(don't call it a wound ... an inner desperate magic
that my child-brain conjured because of some lack,

a need to flee ...). Insect wings shimmer in the hos-
pice parking lot lights. I hear antennae brush against

the light's aura, a composition that keeps spiraling
deeper into itself, shocking and illusive as the hand

that suddenly reaches out of the tree, touches the back
of my neck, sends a shiver through my body (don't

call it a wound, call it a window, a broken window,
that lets so much in ...)

Ancestor, Bringing the World
Continually into Being

She struggles through a water-slick crevice, emerges
in another cave. I wake. But she continues, deeper into

the dream, runs her hands across stone, blind, inside
earth's belly, waits for the creature at the end of her

fingers to move with her touch, begin to stir, feeling
how the darkness moves, speaks. She lights a torch,

gives the creature eyes, sees how it stares back at her,
recognizing itself. She mixes crushed limestone and fat;

haematite and sap. She spits into the paint, mixes herself
into the color, begins the arc of the horse's head, paints

the eyes, the moment when the colt broke from the herd,
moved towards her, mapped her curiosity and fear by

smell, and entered this dream, each hair on its body an
antenna, sensitive to the shift of starlight. Charcoal

blackens her fingers, and she looks into the horse's eyes,
alive inside her, looking back at her, returning her to leaf,

ravine, water, blood, the living, the dead.

Rain, The Ceaseless Sea, The Water Works Drowned, and Prophesy: How the World Was Made

Ever since the flood, the long Cassandra scream.
Balls of water for nine months, smashing onto

concrete, roofs, battering leaves, then water
suddenly everywhere lapped up to the highway's

shoulder as we drove pell-mell into the city
before the water cut us off from home. Sea north,

south, soy and corn waving beneath water like
kelp. Ever since the flood, Cassandra pleading,

this is coming, this is coming soon everywhere,
but it wasn't soon enough and so was laughed at,

chicken-littled, forgotten. Cars floated, entranced
in brown foam, then disappeared, like morning

dreams. Water surrounded and drowned the water
works: no water in the taps, only buckets of rain-

water to flush the shit, long lines at the national
guard water distribution centers, in the rain,

the ceaseless sea. Ever since the flood, the exhaust-
tion from Cassandra's cursed pleading, then her

long sink into havoc. You remember? There was
rain until my body was rain; and your body was rain,

too, beating against your desperate desire to share
this prophetic fear, of what you knew was coming

everywhere. And I watched a father and four-year-
old daughter in the street, in the rain, the ceaseless

sea, as he squeezed shampoo onto the girl's head,
in the rain, the ceaseless sea, and lathered her hair,

the girl laughing and laughing, her eyes closed
against the soap, all roads in and out under water,

her head tipped up to the rain, the ceaseless sea,
laughing.

What Is Crow (Polyphony)

Crows fill the bare maples, between baroque trills and
iron-crust-against-plaster croaks, they dip their heads,
swipe beaks, black to cold branch: *What is wood?* Wood

was one of the solutions soil came up with when it was
asked to invent the sky. *And what is sky?* The gravity
source that pulled black wings out of crow bodies, that

now whirl and scatter and land on the rehab lawn across
the street. Their claws break the surface, look for inver-
tebrates, who repeat over and over in their sleep *What*

is root? The bridge between sorrow and crushed stone,
annihilation of form being the first loss, still preserved
in the grey winter light reflected off a crow's eye, asking

What is night? A loosely linked multi-organ animal,
sometimes mistaken for jellyfish in drowning dreams,
that feeds off the mystery of borders, constantly search-

ing for the place where it might begin and end. *Is it with*
elk? Their hunger inside a hemlock shadow? *Is it with*
wolf lichen? A net that filters the blood of poisoned and

resentful spirits that hide in valley fog? *Is it with bat?* A
way to map seemingly empty space using insect bodies
and their atonal wings? In the morning there was a thin

layer of snow. Crow companion-calls echoed off nearby
walls: *What is crow?* A crocus poking through the ice.
What is crow? A bee rising from the purple-yellow petal

cup. *What is crow?* A woman in a wheelchair, inhaling
cigarette smoke. *What is crow?* A hummingbird huddled
on a bare branch, cold.

Cairn: Earth and Mother

1

Hail beats glass. Waves beat stone stacks. I press
my palm to the window, feel the thousand impacts

scatter through my skin; tiny waves slice into and
slide through my body—bacteria, desert sand part-

icles from half a world away, microplastics . . . So
many deaths, She says (Earth—here, now—inside

me). They sound the depths, resonate through each
cell, demand to be seen, heard, felt. I feel the absence

burrow deep into the liver, the heart, my hand and
rib bones, the space between joints, my face.

2

Waves reach up into the falling hail, can't find a
hold, fall back into foam. She's gone, and I'm left

with the absence she passed on to me so long ago
(Decades since I referred to her as "my mother").

Young and drunk, I once said, you say the same
two things about your childhood, what really hap-

pened to you? Drunk, too, she erupted as if I had
violated a vow of silence I didn't know I'd made.

A vow to that absence, that I held for her, against
her, denied existed, fought with, tried to ignore.

3

Grey light in the east. Christmas lights hang from
a balcony on the hillside. Hail becomes rain and

rain dissolves the ice stones scattered on concrete
and sand. She says: my fingers are dark with know-

ledge of how to coax the voice of flies, dead rabbits
lying roadside, a lizard's husk, the ghosts of parents

who lost their children, up from the breath-holes in
sand, appearing as the wave sinks back into the sea.

She tells me how end-patterns flow: shrivel-lines of
a turtle carcass, silence that follows the owl's glide.

4

I keep forgetting. After her death, I went days
without thinking of her. One memory returned:

how I grabbed her hand during a parade in
Livorno, terrified of the crowd's crush, knowing

she'd shake my hand off. For some reason she held
on, for so long while I stared, suddenly safe, trans-

fixed by those massive papier-maché heads; for so
long, until I turned, to a young woman, smiling

down at me, surprised, amused. I let go, humiliated,
terrified, and ran: absence chasing absence.

5

She says I am here, have always been here: I am
the hagfish, first slime eel, who spins dark out of

dark, with twisted sarcophagus gullet, jawless, spine-
less, spraying viscoelastic mucus, masking everything

in shadow, opaque shapes that set evolution into hip-
grinding motion. She says: I am the nematode worm,

mephisto worm, devouring bacterial slime—dead
parts of the earth—two miles beneath the surface in

gold mines fit only for angels made from pain and
hunger. I have been here all this time.

6

I find a rubbery bullwhip kelp stalk, wave it like
a wand, write spells in sand. Lines and circles: sea-

weed runes that try and wake mole crabs from
their winter sleep, help me remember her eyes,

so green, full of rage; how I fled to a nearby
swamp to hide from that rage: inside a hollow

oak trunk, dead wood curving around me, still
alive with ants, centipedes, tiny stars from

the dim light reflected in the eyes of a thousand
recently hatched spiders.

7

She says: my mouth is the black-red hollyhock,
mourner's flower, that will replace the heart,

the liver, the spleen, after death. She says: I measure
how the mass of the flower's entrails draw everything

into its orbit. She says: I open my hands and there
is a grey sky, sound of scattered rain on sand all day,

same sound as the last breath: that strange softness
that rises from the body's heave, throwing the soul

back into the world, to merge, ride the back of an
unmoored bullwhip kelp stalk to shore.

8

I remember how her eyes shifted between rage and
gone-away, how I followed her into that absence,

learned to hook my hand on a ghost dolphin's fin,
swim through the cold; breathe underwater for days;

transform into a bearded catfish, able to speak with
colors that slip along grass spider webs, break

the surface, float out the bedroom window, circle
past the Moon, Mars, Andromeda's million million

stars. Like her, I always found it hard to mark the line
where memory ends and imagination begins.

9

She says: images are part of the body's memory, story
stored in muscles, nerves, organs; how the oak's bare

branches twist, climb, roots moving toward moving
grey clouds, a pattern that reveals that what's gone is

still here, weaving through earth and sky, right now,
right here. She says: look at the kelp still carrying its

anchor, stone filmed with a calcium carbonate crust,
past exposed on the sand. She points at a woman and

dog further down the beach: look at how she walks,
accompanied by both her past and her death.

10

A short video sent the night before she died, how
her eyes wandered the room, gathered in movement:

great-grandchildren, children. Did she finally feel
their attention? The girl's face I always saw was

gone, the face that endlessly waited for someone to
hold her, keep her safe; bear the burden of the child's

cruel optimism, always on the brink of *something
good*, smiling now at long-dead cats, poinsettia petals

falling like snowflakes, spray off the crest of a break-
ing wave, all there to witness her crossing.

11

She tells me to pick up a stone, listen. What do you
hear? I say: Wind? She puts the stone to her ear:

I hear a lost ocean, children's voices, termites dream-
ing, asphodels brushing against each other's gowns.

She hands the stone back, says: stack them, feel their
mass in your palms. I pick up a stone, listen: a child

who felt the fear inside his mother's body, and re-
fused to take a first breath. She picks up a stone, says:

this is the last passenger pigeon, her body holds an
absence the size of an empty sky.

12

A seagull stabs a crab in the shallows, drags it from
the water upside down, breaks the underbelly, picks

at still-alive meat. Grey hair flies at the corner of my
eye: another witness. I remember she once gave me

a children's book about an artist obsessed with white
swans, pursued them until he froze to death, became

a swan himself. Why that book? The other witness
watches new gulls arrive, carries her story in her

attention, her stance; the way I carry mine in how I
keep my distance.

13

I build a small cairn. I say: this smooth, black
stone is a girl who found love swimming with deep-

sea fish. This half sand dollar is a Fender's Blue
Butterfly, circling, circling, finding no mate. This

orange and brown stone is a run-away, plucked off
the street by a crow, discarded on this beach, living

where he was abandoned. This green sea-glass is a
sea turtle suffocating in a fishing trawl. I suddenly

hold my breath: to keep from being discovered by
the absence moving all around me, restless.

14

Further down the beach, two girls hunt for things to
take home: shells, sea glass, sand dollars. I imagine

her doing this with some friend in her youth, curious,
talking non-stop, in awe of all the strange and beaut-

iful architecture scattered on the sand. A woman
offers local knowledge to the girls about where to

find huge starfish—on the far side of several rocks
just now swamped by the rising tide. The girls ven-

ture out, but the tide's too high now, too cold, and
they retreat, frustrated and laughing.

15

I find half a mussel shell, nacre revealing secrets
of the underworld's sky, put it to my ear: a child

drifts across the moon, nudged on by the moonfish's
blind snout, believing it has bumped into its own

soul. I find a stone with two pits bored by anemones
or water or both, with a tiny black stone stuck in one.

I put my ear to the blocked hole: a spotted frog calls
out, waits to hear a response that may never come.

She says: where does that cry come from, where can
it find a home?

16

Where is she now? I remember one moment, ten
years ago, when she emerged from her confused

fog, said: "We all have feelings, some just don't
show it." So much turmoil she was forced to hide

from herself, from us, for so long, until it exhaust-
ed her brain, her body. The cairn will be gone to-

morrow. I see sorrow, cradled inside a mussel's
half shell, slip off the continental shelf and fall,

towards her, on the ocean floor, watching how un-
dulating bioluminescence becomes a ferry's light.

17

She says: I will find her one of these mornings,
wandering before dawn, and I will take her hand,

enfold it within my own bones; begin a chant that
envelops and transforms fear, holds the promise

of finally being held, surrounded by soil, shell,
worm, beetle, stones inside stones—the promise

of weight, of that longed-for embrace, that con-
nects her to each thin root-thread, dividing hunger

from desire; connects her to the sea star's speckled
surface, prototype of the night sky.

18

Seven pelicans dip towards the water, one behind
the other, sail on the aircushion their wings make,

ride the wave's curl, until it breaks, and they peel
off. Spray flies from the wave's crest, dissolves

into grey mist. I stretch out my arms, turn in a
circle on the sand, edge of a wave's reach; turn

slowly, through so much dying, absence: dead
zone off the coast; mussels boiled in their own

shells from last summer's heat, clinging to a
tangle of tossed earbud wires at my feet.

19

I turn and She calls on the dead—the seen, here
on the beach; the unseen, always moving just out

of reach—to help shape my turning, with their
salt arms, salt embrace, surrounding me with

salt's fire; wrap each memory in salt water, salt
and wonder; salt that quickens the transmission

of nerve impulses, repeats the pattern of star-
birth inside galactic clouds across the body; salt

that grounds the charge of sorrow, confusion,
into shifting caverns of salt beneath me.

20

More rain, and I stop turning, face the sea,
the surrounding absence; an absence I share

with the sea stacks braced against relentless
waves; with the waves turning a half-gutted

fish in the shallows; with a green anemone de-
vouring a snail whole; with everything forged

of salt and hunger, salt and longing; an absence
I share with her, my mother. The dark head of a

seal appears in the aftermath of a wave, slips
under the surface of churning brown foam . . .

Ancestors

1

I woke from a dream of unformed shadows,
rising from the earth, reaching out—and saw
thousands of oak leaves fly by, torn out of
the sky, into the sky.

2

In the morning, the oak was bare. I found two
oak leaves on the balcony. For one second, I
thought they were ochre hand-prints, blown
onto the concrete.

3

I placed my hands next to the leaves.

Notes

Pg 21. "Starry Night over the Rhone (Vincent van Gogh)"

"Night is richer in color than the day." This line is from a van Gogh letter to his brother while he was working on this painting. (*Van Gogh, The Complete Paintings*, Taschen, 2020)

Pg 32. "Our Mother's Body"

The years listed are historical plague/pandemic dates: 1347, Black Death/Europe and Mediterranean;1665, Plague of London; 1899, Black Plague Epidemic in the Territory of Hawaii, spread from the Mumbai Plague Epidemic that struck that city in 1896. The date 1918 references the Great Influenza Epidemic (1918–1920) that killed an estimated 500 million people worldwide.

Enola Gay is the name of the plane that dropped the first atomic bomb on Hiroshima.

Pg 40. "Nacer de Nuevo/Rebirth (Remedios Varo)"

"*Luminar* as *Liminar*"—the connection between Luminar and Liminar was derived in part from an article about Varo's work by Ricki O'Rawe and Roberta Ann Quance, "Crossing the Threshold: Mysticism, Liminality, and Remedios Varo's *Bordando el manto terrestre*," 1961–62. The article discusses Varo's protagonists/heroines as liminars, characters who are on their way to initiation into esoteric knowledge, on the threshold; taken from Victor Turner's conception of the liminal. Luminar is derived from a combination of related words in English and Spanish, referencing "luminary," "body of light," and "genius."

Pg 41. "Low"

"Nutria" and "yellow heart" are both invasive species.

Pg. 42. "Car Batteries, Falling Snow, Snakestones"

"This is the way we take care of each other now," is taken from the insightful question: "Is this the way we take care of each other now?" asked by Hilary Hildebrand when I mentioned that my battery was stolen but the thieves didn't do any damage to the car.

Pg 49. "Ancestors, Day of Dead"

Labyrinth of Solitude is a work by the Mexican poet Octavio Paz, a book of essays primarily concerned with Mexican identity. It was published in the 1950s.

Pg 52. "Two Turkey Vultures: Early Spring"

The "she" in the poem is a composite of my biological mother and an imagined earth/death mother. This theme is further developed in "Cairn: Earth and Mother."

Pg 55. "Watching Apricot Blossoms Fly during a Time of Plague"

Superstitious cures listed at the beginning of the poem in italics are from the European Middle Ages. The last one listed is a variation on various superstitions that were circulated during the height of the Covid pandemic in the United States.

"No virus. Hoax." This quote is verbatim. I was lying in a room, with a fever from Covid, when I overheard a conversation taking place on the street below my window about the virus being a conspiratorial hoax.

Pg. 57. "Dragonfly in the Palm"

"It's greenish-yellow compound eyes rove across my face, divine thirty different pigments . . ." Humans have tri-chromatic vision—seeing colors as combinations of red, blue, and green—due to three different types of light-sensitive proteins called opsins. Many dragonfly species have eleven light-sensitive proteins, and some have thirty such proteins. I imagined this ability to see a significantly wider spectrum of color to be the kind of vision a god would have.

Pg. 67. "The Disappeared"

This poem started out in the voice of pure fear, referencing those "disappeared" by the US government to black sites around the world in its ongoing "war on terror." Eventually, I expanded it to include those reported missing in the continental US due to human trafficking and child abduction, including the terrifying crisis of missing and murdered indigenous people.

Pg 73. "Rain, The Ceaseless Sea, The Water Works Drowned, and Prophesy: How the World Was Made"

This poem references the flood of 1993 in Des Moines, Iowa, a taste of what was to come on a regular basis around the world thirty years later due to the climate crisis/emergency.

Pg 76. "Cairn: Earth and Mother"

This poem moves back and forth between communication with Earth as mother (encompassing both life and death aspects) in the present and memories related to my mother:

"... bacteria, desert sand particles from half a world away, microplastics..." A small list of the possible particulate composition inside a hail stone.

"... a children's book about an artist obsessed with white swans..." A reference to the book The Painter and the Wild Swans by Claude Clement (author) and Frederic Clement (illustrator), Dial, 1986.

CHRISTIEN GHOLSON is the author of several books of poetry, including *Absence : Presence* (Shanti Arts Publishing) and *All the Beautiful Dead Along the Side of the Road* (Bitter Oleander Press); along with a novel: *A Fish Trapped Inside the Wind* (Parthian Books). Several chapbooks can be found online, including *Tidal Flats* (Mudlark). He attended Naropa University; University of California, Davis; and Southwestern College in Santa Fe, New Mexico. His work has appeared in *Alaska Quarterly Review, Banyan Review, Ecotone, Flyway, Hotel Amerika, Mudlark, Permafrost, The Shore, The Sun,* and *Tiger Moth Review,* among many other literary journals, and is the recipient of a Pushcart Prize. He works as a somatic-oriented mental health counselor at a clinic collective. He lives in Eugene, Oregon, where he is engaged in an endless dialogue about birth and death with a local murder of crows. christiengholson.blogspot.com

SHANTI ARTS

NATURE ▪ ART ▪ SPIRIT

Please visit us online
to browse our entire book catalog,
including poetry collections and fiction,
books on travel, nature, healing, art,
photography, and more.

Also take a look at our highly regarded art
and literary journal, *Still Point Arts Quarterly*,
which may be downloaded for free.

www.shantiarts.com